The Human Side of

Lean Enterprise

By Alan R. Severance

"If It's Lean,

It's Routine"

Contents

Acknowledgements and Thanks

I have to thank a world of people who make this book come to life for me, especially:

Rick Cooper, Bernie Currie, Dick Jordan, Lee Ozley, Terry Reiss, and Mel Silver, the leaders and manufacturing professionals who mentored, guided, cajoled, and pushed me to learn how to lead people and have fun in manufacturing.

Darnall Daley, a fellow APICS board member, whose insight and book critique were especially valuable.

The entire staff at Feather River Door Company for providing the perfect laboratory to practice and improve everything I learned about people and leadership, and especially Todd

Pleasants, arguably the best plant manager in the Northeast.

Jon Sharp, a true Theory L Leader, a good friend, the sharpest critic and best student I ever had.

My partners at Riverton, Kathy Crowley and Dr. Miles Overholt, who are my sounding board and editors.

David Grubb, a most unique engineer – one who has written and spoken as much on the human side of Lean as he has on the technical side.

Dedication

I dedicate this book to the greatest family in the world: my wife Diane, our children Julie, Jeff, and Teresa, my brother Dick, and Pop, all of whom taught me about people and about life. Thank you all. I love you all.

Leadership for the 21st Century

I wrote this book to convince you of two things. First, your organization must become Lean to survive and thrive in this century. Second, the best way to become Lean is to find as many other leaders as you can within your organization to train as leaders and facilitators of Continuous Improvement Teams. I call these people Theory L leaders.

Thanks to Douglas McGregor, author of The Human Side of Enterprise, we know those who believe that people want to contribute to and enjoy their jobs are Theory Y people; people who understand people and work to help others achieve their goals. I maintain, though, that new organizational leaders must be more than that. The people who really understand the Lean transformation and how best to continuously improve I call Theory L people. Their goal is not only to behave as good Theory Y managers, but is also to create as many more good, people-oriented managers as possible so that the pool of good leaders is greatly enlarged throughout the organization and the pool of good followers are team players.

Douglas McGregor coined the terms Theory X and Theory Y to explain the differences he saw in types of managers. He noted that some managers continued along a centuries-old path, thinking that since they were in charge, they must know everything and had to dictate not just what had to be done but how it must be done, as well. Micromanagement was born well before the Roman Empire! Others adopted a more enlightened or democratic mode, believing that since they didn't know everything, they would use the minds and experience of their employees as well as their own to solve problems or decide future direction for opportunity

To a young part-time MBA student, these descriptions seemed more like a choice of pathways to leadership, and since I knew what kind of leader I preferred, I consciously set out to become a Theory Y manager. I will leave to others to describe how well I achieved this, but I worked very hard to follow this philosophy.

As I grew into roles with increasing amounts of responsibility, I knew I had to rely increasingly on the knowledge and experience of others to learn each new job and to succeed at it. I also had to support my own growth by ensuring that I could be replaced in my current job if I were to be considered for another. I began to watch my subordinates for behaviors that showed me they respected and understood others and could find ways to help them succeed. I then made sure that those I thought were good leaders got additional training and experience in the managerial aspects of the job as well. A good manager isn't always a good leader, but a good leader must be a good - or good enough - manager to get things done in the context of the overall organization he or she works in.

The philosophy of Just-In-Time seemed to be a natural extension of Theory Y: use Continuous Improvement Teams to make processes, and the workplace itself, better for all those using them. As JIT evolved into Lean and began to encompass entire organizations, I was again an "early adapter" and eagerly adopted the principles. Reduced set-up time, shorter cycle time, cellular manufacturing and flow all made a great deal of sense to me. Making changes in the plant layout, shortening lead times for product, reducing inventory were all exciting to accomplish. All are very measurable and it was fun to track progress. We all like to get good report cards!

Of course, there were multiple hiccups in implementations. We had to shelve a great idea in changing our upholstery process because our spray booth was an anchor – putting another hole in a perfectly good roof is not something to be undertaken lightly, and who knew what other bumps we would hit on the regulatory and environmental side if we moved our grandfathered exhaust stack. We went back to the drawing board and came up with less than optimum solutions that were still much better than our starting point.

Another time, our planned warehouse reorganization was halted by corporate's unwillingness to allow neither the disruption to service nor the proposed costs of better retrieval equipment despite an excellent ROI. We knew we were on the right track, however, so we re-thought the layout and arrived at a different configuration that gave us 75% of what we wanted without any capital expenditure or loss of service.

These are just two real-world examples of a determined team finding ways to gain some improvement in process despite roadblocks to a potentially optimum solution. After all, neither Lean nor Continuous Improvement are projects; they are all about incremental improvement as an on-going way of life.

And of course, other issues developed as the workforce balked at some of the changes. While many people wanted to accept the promise of making their jobs easier, others were fearful of changes to accepted norms and procedures. While everyone was somewhere on the change-now vs. the don't-change continuum, they were all at different points of readiness to accept. Individual facilitators and their teams dealt with these issues differently and with widely varied results. Some worked hard to show reluctant comrades that the ideas were good. Some teams were so badly split that little was accomplished. My own frustration grew exponentially.

Forced to think about the successes and the failures, I concluded that, overall, there was provable success. Even where walls (roofs!) or lack of capital blocked the initially desired solution, determination and imagination pushed past the disappointment and allowed committed people to make improvements anyway. But where the impediments were the people themselves, there were no significant changes.

I wish I could say that I had an "Aha!" moment, but in truth it took some more years for me to see the real problem. The Continuous Improvement Teams that succeeded had leaders who understood the facilitator role. They took advantage of the support they earned by their respect and trust of the team members to move them past the usual resistance-to-change factor. They used the team's own expertise to prove out new processes and changes. They began to look to the natural leaders and communicators on each team as allies in making things happen. The best of the facilitators would bring me names of people they thought would make good team leaders.

I deliberately began to expand the number of team leaders/facilitators so that more teams could be employed. We taught problem-solving skills, meeting management, and the use of spaghetti charts to find some of the Seven Wastes. We taught them that there was an Eighth Waste – overlooking the skills, abilities, and experience of the other team members!

I began to think that the best way to succeed in a Lean initiative was to cascade the attitude throughout the organization that every team leader's job was to find and grow more leaders. The more who understood WHY we wanted to be Lean, the more success we achieved at the team level. And the more success we had, the more we wanted additional teams working on their own solutions to the things that frustrated them every day, the things that they found de-motivating or discouraging.

Leaders in manufacturing companies adopt Lean Manufacturing as their operating philosophy for some or all of the many reasons amply discussed over the last thirty years. Those who really understand its power have driven it to become the culture of their plants and warehouses. Lean at its best is simply "the way we do things around here." The advantages of a Lean company over its non-Lean rivals are many and are usually reduced to a dollars and cents presentation because that is the acknowledged business scorecard: did our profit increase as a result of Lean and by how much?

Too often overlooked is the contribution that Lean Leadership makes to the creation of an environment that empowers workers, creates opportunities, encourages contribution, and rewards both individual and team efforts to continuously improve.

Lean initiatives succeed when they create this new breed of leader.

In my ideal world, these would all be Theory Y leaders. Then I realized successful leaders had to be more than that.   They had to be Theory Y leaders who could recognize the next generation of leaders and begin their training. Those who know this and know why it is important are the new Theory L leaders.

Chapter One: Why I Want You to Read This Book, Have Fun, and Become a Theory L Leader.

Getting Lean is the current engine of change in organizations of every kind. It is the application of a relentless search for and the active elimination of waste wherever it is found in every part of any enterprise. Properly done, it is an opportunity for everyone involved to share in results ranging from reduced frustration on the job, to increased job satisfaction created by the opportunity to contribute to success.

Lean can be done top-down. It has been done by management looking to spruce up a company to make it look better to potential buyers. It has been done by desperate companies trying to understand how someone else ate their lunch, leaving no scraps behind. It can be done in isolated pockets of larger organizations, creating some improvements for these segments. In other words, Theory X and Theory Y managers alike can create a Lean initiative. So why do I want you to do something else? Because, while any of the above might be necessary in the short run, it is absolutely no fun to go Lean as just described!

Becoming Lean means changing your culture to change the attitudes, behaviors, and habits of the entire workforce to support a philosophy of continuous improvement. And this really is great fun because you can see the results immediately as you proceed! Those engaged in this change process will create a more robust organization, one much more likely to succeed. If you can provide the best product or service or cost, people will buy from you and not your competitors, providing the only real job security anyone in the private sector has.

Again, with appropriate apologies to Douglas McGregor, I call this Theory L leadership. It is more than just Theory Y, although you must start with Theory Y leaders, those who value the people in an organization. These leaders must then deliberately teach leadership to as many people as possible at every level of an organization, not just exhibit the best leadership at the top. In this way, the positive changes in attitude, behavior, and culture required to sustain a solid Lean organization become the norm for the entire workforce.

What do you get in return for this? You get a safe working environment in which engaged workers produce high quality products or services at a price your customers will willingly pay.

Lean initiatives succeed when they create this new breed, the Theory L Leader. Why?

Well, from your personal experience, tell me: Which of the following initiatives are technologically oriented or people oriented?

1. Safety.

2. Quality.

3. Productivity.

If you answered "Yes!" you are correct! It really is "all the above" and there are no trade-offs allowed any more. You must succeed with all three of these categories to succeed as an organization.

All of our initiatives, our attempts to create better organizations in manufacturing or any other industry, involve the interaction of new or different ways of doing things with the people we count on to get the job done.

So you must go Lean to succeed, to stay in business, and to make money. What path do you take to get there by the surest method? Continuous Improvement of people, process, and product. Engage your workforce and you will become instantly more competitive. Train your workforce to solve their own problems in teams and you have created the best force multiplier you can think of. Teach as many as you can how to lead small groups and work teams. Leaders will emerge; teach them everything they need to know to lead groups and solve problems, and then jump out of their way.

The results of a people-focused, team-oriented approach to waste elimination will produce almost instant savings for the organization and rewards for those who have risked stepping up to help.

This journey is literally fun and simple, though I caution you not to confuse "simple" with "easy" or you will be greatly disappointed. Create a plan that includes a lot of your time and hard work. Continuous Improvement is, well, continuous, and you are in for the duration.

A word about Lean language, the terms and acronyms I use throughout the book. This book is written for practitioners with knowledge of Lean techniques, so I have not stopped to define or explain every word that forms the language of Lean. This book is not meant to be your first introduction to Lean or Lean practices. I will, however, give enough of a definition to help with the context and give you a start on looking up further information if you require. In addition, I reference Dr. Elihu Goldratt, author of The Goal, his ground-breaking book on his Theory of Constraints, and his now famous symbol for a bottleneck in a process flow: Herbie, the boy whose position in the line of hiking scouts impedes the flow of the entire troop in various ways.

In the following chapters I will introduce you to many of the stumbling blocks that you will encounter in a people-centered approach to Lean, and offer some ideas how to change them into building blocks for your own journey to become a Theory L leader. The list won't be complete and the solutions provided for some instances will not work across the board, so you must stay alert, stay in the moment, and deal with the reality you face. And as I have said, if you are not having fun, you are not doing it right! Take a deep breath. Start!

Chapter Two – Top Management Commits – Or Else!

I am convinced that the road to Lean is a necessary journey for every organization, but it is not always a straight and smooth path. While countless books and websites tell you how to do Lean, most do not offer help where it is needed most – when something goes wrong on the people side. I do not know of any Lean implementation failures caused by technical issues. When people are determined to improve, they find a way. Even if circumstances or lack of capital prevent the optimum solution, determined people will take an action that lets them implement a solution to revise processes or improve situations

And I have seen that where the human side is ignored or down-played, problems arise that can slow or stop a Lean implementation. What happens to an initiative if top management does not buy in? Ah! We have found our first impediment!

I make a practice of beginning Lean implementation at the top of an organization, and I do this by presenting an "Owner's Manual" for Lean. Right from the start, I want to know if I have complete and active buy-in from the company's executive leadership. Everybody likes the idea of eliminating waste and reducing non-value added activities. The best leaders understand that this is their job. Many others want the same outcomes but don't commit to personalizing the new philosophy. Those who think that Lean is a project will find someone to manage it for them. They will then wonder why they have realized so few of the benefits that the books or consultants told them they would see.

Leadership from the top provides the best opportunity to succeed, for this or any initiative, and I always do my best to create an understanding why this is necessary. I start with the usual definitions of Lean, Waste, and Non-Value Added. I present Toyota's classic list of the Seven Wastes (rework, over production, over processing, waiting, moving, transporting, and excess inventory) and then make sure they also understand the Eighth Waste as most often added by US practitioners – management overlooking the intelligence and skills of their employees. I tell executives that the rules for success continue to change, creating a need for Theory L people, people who can lead and also teach leadership, in order to respond to changes as they happen.

All of the people working in an organization have a stake in its success and continued existence, and most will jump at the chance to help improve because they know that providing better service or better products is the ONLY way to get job security. They are not thinking about stock prices, executive bonuses or other short-term goals. They want to pay off the mortgage, send kids to college, afford reliable cars, and take a vacation once in a while. They want the company to succeed this year and every year until they retire.

Sometimes it takes a serious amount of convincing, usually by a mix of education, the experience of other companies, and potential results to get commitment. And what if Top Management doesn't buy in? Should you give up or find a way to proceed? Don't give up without a fight, if you are on the inside.

One proven way to win senior executives over is to pilot a Lean effort and show the results. Carefully plan this effort to show what can be accomplished by using a little directed teamwork. Of course you will pick a project that gives a quick payback with negligible expense. Even companies that have made previous attempts to be Just-In-Time or Lean will have many opportunities to show improvement in cost or quality or both.

It is usually hard for owners and senior management to ignore success, and they will want to see more, making this the best time to introduce or reintroduce a company-wide Lean initiative that now has active support from the top.

When the Lean philosophy is adopted as the way of life in a people-centered environment, the organization will enjoy markedly better results from the behaviors and mindsets of all who are involved.

No buy-in at all? No support for even a trial run to see if you succeed or fall flat on your face? No one respects your skill enough to let you try something this important? Well, then, this is your personal version of "Or else!" because it now gets very easy for you! Find someone to work for who respects your skills and shares your philosophy! You will be so much happier spending ten or twelve energized hours a day at the new place than going home after squeaking through eight hours just as frustrated as when you came to work. Your departure will not help your current company's executives; you will be the topic of conversation when they next meet, and one of them will say, "See! I TOLD you that if we train people they'll leave!"

Don't look back and don't worry about them. They will have all their untrained people with them when they line up for unemployment.

Where the owners or senior execs buy in, Lean will transform the company as corporate goals actually get transferred into action plans. Lean companies bring new products on line quicker, make better products more cost effectively in a safer work environment, and accomplish the desired improvements in profitability, market share, and customer satisfaction. In the office, Lean companies streamline paper work and reduce lead times, ensuring a faster cash-to-cash cycle as the ability to invoice sooner for each order is sped up.

Once the management team is on board, we can assure the rest of the people that their Lean efforts will be appreciated. We can now ask them to contribute their ideas and efforts to success.

Chapter Three- It IS Your Job

Lean succeeds the quickest when it is cascaded down through the organization, so we must now introduce all managers and supervisors to Lean concepts and create a Theory L environment for them to work in. In some ways, this is more difficult than getting the senior management buy-in.

The biggest show-stopper of any major initiative is failure of the front line supervision to buy into it, and Lean is not exempt from this. There are many ways these key leaders can derail your efforts, and for many reasons. Some will feel threatened if asked to give up control to a team or work group; others lack the people skills required to succeed in the new way. Some will feel inadequate to lead and facilitate. Some can't give up their comfort zone of just "hitting the numbers" for today or this week or this month. And some will think you are not serious about changing, that you are just giving them more work to do that is unrelated to their current work paradigm.

How do you address this problem? First, check to see that you haven't created your own monster. If you have been pushing them all to make their production numbers, a supervisor might need extra coaching just to understand that you do really mean that getting Lean is now more important than today's schedule. Is this a tough message? Yes! You have to take the necessary communication steps to introduce the need for change and assure everyone that you will never penalize a schedule shortfall caused by stopping production to make a change, hold a team meeting, or solve a problem. And you have to stick to message even if you know that a critical order may be falling behind or that the shop might have to work overtime to complete this week's schedule!

You can overcome other concerns with training and education. Give supervisors the skills they will need to succeed in the new way. Teach them how to facilitate a meeting and to solve a problem with a team. Coach the supervisors to help them understand that Lean will make their jobs easier. They no longer have to solve every problem or overcome every issue by themselves. There will be those who truly don't understand why you insist on going Lean, or who will wonder what is "behind" this new initiative. Keep telling them the truth. Show them that it is the new way of life with every message you give to them.

Most importantly, give them a job, a role within the transition that engages them and teaches them at the same time. Coach them to lead some of the training exercises; give them huge rolls of red tape to find all the items in a given area or workstation that do not meet 5S standards. Keep them busy until they realize that they are leading part of the change, selling it to colleagues and subordinates alike.

Create a culture for supervisors that applauds risks and mistakes. When they are no longer worried about screwing up, they will be much more likely to come up with creative ideas to move their teams forward. Tell them it's OK to try their ideas or their team's ideas as fast as they can implement them. The faster they succeed, after all, the more they are likely to keep moving in the direction you want. And the faster they fail, the quicker they will be able to try something else!

Above all, get the front-line people to understand that Lean is What-They-Do, not what they do after they complete today's schedule. Lean is their job now, and that now means being Lean, leading Lean teams, and identifying and training the next set of Lean leaders. This is Theory L!

This effort will help you get most of the people on board, those that can deal with change, adopt new ideas quickly, or can be coached into a hands-on position. What will you do with the managers and supervisors who do not step up?

First, let's identify those who might not follow. I worked with two reluctant supervisors at one client. Both gave great answers in class, both enthusiastically responded to my ideas and suggestions. Both ignored me and everything we discussed when they were on the shop floor.

We began most implementations with 5 S, the Toyota model for creating a safe, orderly, productive workspace. The Japanese words begin with an S, so some of the translations are a little loose in order to retain the S's: Sort, Straighten Up, Shine, Standardize, Sustain. Hey, it's what your Mom always told you: A place for everything and everything in its place!

The first supervisor I refer to above simply did not want to do the work necessary to change; she was very comfortable doing things the same tomorrow as she did yesterday because it worked yesterday. Things were going well enough. She didn't have to spend much time with the line and she liked being the boss! I know you don't have anyone like this in your shop, but if you did, you might wonder what to do with such an impediment to your Lean effort. This type of person will need one-on-one time with you outside the classroom. She will need repeated assurance that you intend to change, that she will have to change with you, and this change is not optional. If she finally gets it, pull her back into the regular training cycle and proceed.

The second supervisor simply took no action to translate the tools that he seemed to understand so well in class to his production area. I spent time on his line and he was able to tell me how to make improvements in his 5S. He could show me where his line could be shortened, offering serious advantages in simplifying staffing and communications. He could do everything except stop production, gather his team and speak to them. I gave him opportunities in class to lead meetings and he did fine. We shut down his line and I watched him facilitate a problem solving session quite nicely, with very little coaching from me. But he could not or would not do it on his own. And he continued to worry about his "numbers," certain that output would still be the most important result at the end of the day. Not only had this been drilled into him since day one, the throughput displays mounted over the end of the lines shouted to him. He knew what the total should be at every hour if he was to meet the daily number for that shift! His boss needed a quick way to capture daily output to create the new metrics (we'll get to that in the next chapter) so he kept the counters in place, all of which he repeatedly explained to this supervisor, but to no avail. In the end, the supervisor left, unable to accept the change.

At another company, one of the supervisors insisted to his crew that "they" (senior management) want to create a 5 S organization. He posted the list of the 5 S steps for all to see and told his staff to get to work on it, after carefully explaining again that "they" want it. He did not remain long with the organization. A poor supervisor to begin with, plant management was quick to move on replacing him with a more people-centered supervisor.

What happens if every effort you make to reach a nonconforming supervisor is rebuffed by that individual? You will have to remove such a person from supervising or from the company if there is no buy-in to the program. If you do not, you risk establishing a double standard, or worse – creating confusion among those who did buy in and are working hard to achieve the Lean goals they now believe in. Someone who doesn't want to actively help lead the change must be taken out of the process and given something else to do or must be let go. If you keep such a person in a key place in your Lean implementation, you immediately send the wrong message to everyone else. The other supervisors and your production people already know who doesn't "get it." They are just wondering if you know and have the courage to do what is right for the organization.

Take good care of your supervisors, give them tools and lots of latitude, make them understand that their job now is to get Lean, and then get out of their way. The rewards for them and for the organization will be overwhelming.

Chapter 4 - Putting Some Fun into Lean!

One of the first "people problems" to arise with any big change initiative is engaging associates immediately. Yes, you will need some class time to introduce the concepts and your purpose, but you then need to get onto the floor as quickly as possible to show everyone the practical side of what they just learned.

If you start with 5S, applying the new concepts is pretty easy. Red tape and red tags become clear visual signals and most people actually enjoy de-cluttering their area or production line or workstation. 5 S becomes the ultimate visual signal for everyone in the area, and 5 S is reinforced by Lean Waste Reduction while maintaining 5 S supports Lean.

Now continue to teach the Eight Wastes in the same visual manner. Grab a big white board and multiple colored makers to make a spaghetti diagram. I know, everyone now calls it Value-stream

Mapping, but I have found it more easily adapted as "spaghetti." While this tool is a "classic", it remains valuable and it can be a lot of fun. It is also an easy tool to use, making the job of the first-time team leader easier, since he or she has no pressure to come up with the starting point for the first session. Facilitators and team leaders will learn how to let the team work things out with just a bit of guidance.

This step couldn't be easier for everyone to learn. The example from Figure 1 is simply a page from my project workbook that I sketched while watching a client's production line. I used it to see how much waste I could find in five minutes of watching. The supervisor and I reviewed the chart and then called the team together to review it. They instantly saw what I saw and the supervisor was able to elicit quite a number of suggestions for eliminating or reducing the walking and waiting associated with the process. The team put several into solutions into practice immediately and the supervisor scheduled some conference room time to plan a revision to the layout on the whiteboards.

For even better results, follow the outline I propose below. I say that it's better because it engages the team right from the beginning.

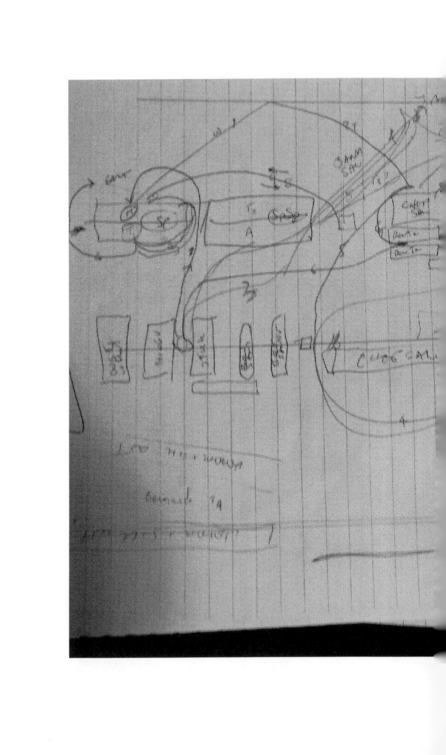

Figure 1

Prepare the event by sketching the warehouse racks or the production lines or the back office layout. One by one, give each team member a colored marker to draw his normal operation sequence and the direction of movement of their product during the course of the job or task. Be sure each member articulates why each movement is necessary. When everyone has had a turn, ask the team to look at the total picture and describe what they see. Who moves the most? Why? Who moves the least? Why? Are there duplicated efforts or movements? Are there redundant activities? Can they identify any of the Eight Wastes?

Begin the discussion about why each movement is currently necessary and whether it can be defined as Value Added or Non-Value Added. If Non-Value Added, which of the Wastes does it represent? Get the team thinking about how each Waste could be eliminated or reduced. Keep the discussion on issues, not people. And keep it light. If this kind of activity isn't fun for the participants, you are just not doing it right! You don't have to tell them that they are "Value-stream Mapping!" They are just having fun.

By the way, Value Added is a concept that is quickly grasped by those introduced to it, no matter their background. A colleague of mine routinely uses the terms to describe Direct and Indirect Labor Costs to his customers' accounting departments. The more you get support departments to use Lean terminology, the easier it becomes to guide them through their own lean initiatives. Waste occurs everywhere!

Now get the team members to describe how their current 5 S efforts have fallen short of full support of their physical workspace. Team members can see some places where supplies or parts should be located when they note that multiple trips or lengthy trips are being made to obtain them because they are not at point of use. See where tools are located or if they are routinely traded during the process; maybe additional tools are needed. Reinforce the lesson by getting any additional tools quickly. You will not only gain some trust by acting on their request quickly, you and the team will immediately see waste being reduced or eliminated.

Take a break now and return to the floor where you can get everyone involved in taking their 5 S to a higher level. You will find that when the team revisits their 5 S effort, they will do so with much greater understanding of the concept and how it relates directly to their daily activities. The team leader can step back here and be the resource and cheerleader. Applaud their efforts; get them more labels and tape; answer the questions; keep a note of problems that cannot be addressed immediately for later resolution by the team.

When you return to the spaghetti chart, be sure to have the team add all the non-routine trips to get parts or supplies or to find the supervisor. This discussion will lead to additional items to be brought closer to the line or more creative ways to accomplish extraneous tasks. They will make great joint problem solving topics with internal suppliers and customers of the team.

This hands-on effort goes a long way to removing the idea that the Lean Initiative is just another "management" gimmick. The team members see the value of the tool and can immediately translate ideas into practical efforts to make their jobs less frustrating. They understand that 5S and Eight Wastes are not abstract classroom ideas but are concrete and fundamental to their Lean efforts. They become more engaged more rapidly because they are at the very center of attention and doing meaningful activity.

This is the point at which I usually introduce Kanbans, because Kanbans can be seen as the next logical step, not another "new" item threatening people. I briefly describe the original Toyota concept of a two-bin system for items used in production, but I tie it into 5 S to make it simply part of what everyone is doing every day. Again, the most important part is making sure the team know the reasons as well as the techniques. It is the team that produces the output, so let them decide where output is staged until needed by their customer. (We'll get back to this in a little bit.)

In the next chapter we will show you how to teach the team to use the schedule or Takt time along with their typical Units/FTE to decide on the size of the Kanbans for each part and supply needed at the line.

What else is fun? Winning! Tackling a tough problem and solving it without kicking it upstairs or running to engineering. Learning to track their efforts and seeing the progress they are making. Learning new things. Defining and designing your own work space. At the next session, use your value stream map by again bringing participants to the white board to list all the steps being currently taken to get the job done. To start, have someone draw a simple layout of the area. As each team member comes to the board to write his sequential list, have him locate his workstation or area on the diagram.

Look at each step to see which of the Eight Wastes occur based on the previous exercise, and determine which can be eliminated or reduced immediately. Then look to see if each person's part of the process takes roughly the same amount of time. Where time study or experience suggest unequal effort, look to see if those with longer tasks can hand off part of their work to their internal supplier or customer. Re-balance the line accordingly and observe or time study the result. Adjust as often as necessary!

Teach the team members to take the time studies. Again, you not only give people more tools, you continue to build the trust that you are using measurements as tools for growth, not punishment. Time studies will overcome perceptions about who works the hardest or which parts of the job are toughest, allowing team members to focus on reducing everyone's effort and the frustrations caused by perception of relative effort. Any time you can remove frustration is a win for the whole team, since this reduction is the second biggest reward you can offer for their help, after the chance to grow professionally.

These tools are extremely useful in creating your team. They are practical, visual, and nonthreatening. You have led the team through several short improvement cycles, building mutual trust and confidence.

You and your team are ready to do even more! You can solve your own problems when your team understands the facts and measurements!

Chapter 5 - Measurements are FOR the People, not ABOUT them!

OK, so if we are here to learn to be good leaders, why are we talking about measurements already? Well, this is not your usual introduction to measurements as a control. It is about teaching more tools to create a smarter, better informed work team that is capable of making many decisions for itself based on clearly understood quantitative measures; simply put, more tools for their tool boxes.

Theory L leaders are going to be asking their teams to track their output, so that the team members can learn to use the data to plan their own work, determine when overtime is necessary, track productivity and quality improvements, and manage the processes under their control. When the team understands the measures and how they are used, they begin to accept the measures for what they are: the practical way to run their part of the business.

They must understand both Takt Time and their cycle time to determine when to ask for more people or more work. Instead of being told of the schedule and expected to complete it, the team will see that these numbers are not arbitrary or burdensome. Numbers simply describe input and output in a business-like way. No one is holding back work from them or loading them up. There is a reason for everything that they are asked to accomplish. This understanding by itself can reduce a lot of frustration for the team. It also lays the ground work for all of the reasoning for employing many of the Lean tools.

The first Lean tool I would include in measurement is Kanbans, defined in their simplest form: a place where something goes. Material coming to a line arrives in a defined quantity and is placed in the designated location. This material is usually gauged to be a sufficient workload for a set period of time, such as two hours, half a shift, or one shift of production. Only this material may be worked on, so it must be of sufficient quantity to last the designated time. There isn't any extra supplied "just in case." Only when the delivered amount is consumed will more work be supplied.

This tool is often used to control inventory, reducing work-in-process amounts or limiting the amount of finished goods produced, but this is backwards.

The difference between dictating Kanban size on inventory grounds alone and teaching the team how to determine the sizes of their own inbound and out bound Kanbans is the key to acceptance of a system that doesn't let them see tons of work at the head of the line. Too often, workers without knowledge equate a pile of work with job security. They haven't been told of the costs of keeping too much Work-In-Process inventory on the shop floor. No one explained that more work is coming, it's just no longer being piled in front of the line" until it's needed. And no one took the time to remind them that job security rests with the customer. Reducing costs and increasing quality secure jobs, not piles of work.

One company I know of implemented Kanban top-down, using the Inventory Planners to decide the Kanban size. The team members accepted this, but then balked at contributing to further reduction of batch size and Kanban size because Kanban size came from "the office" so they couldn't possibly change it.

Another company introduced Kanbans as simply the next step in 5 S. The teams were challenged to determine how much inbound product they needed to meet normal schedules without having too much product on the line or having items replenished so often that material handlers couldn't keep up, stopping production. The teams decided on the quantities of parts needed, determined a location for empty bins, adjusting the area layout and re-lining and relabeling to sustain their 5 S.

When the subject of reducing Kanban sizes was introduced, the team members offered up many ideas and quickly understood the impact on batch sizes. The results included reduction of WIP, of course, but also reduced the lines' footprints which allowed further shortening of the lines. After a quick update of each line's 5 S organization and a re-balance of some of the lines, some staff members were reassigned to areas short of people. From here, the leap to a Pull System became much easier to understand and accomplish.

A second important tool for teams is the concept of FTE, Full Time Equivalent Employees.

Teams learn that adding people to get more product is not always the Lean way to proceed. Teams learn to measure the amount of output per day or per week as a factor of the number of people applied. If U/FTE (Units produced divided by the

Full Time Equivalent employees) drops when more people or overtime hours are applied to get more output, everyone can immediately see what this costs and why the company cannot continue to solve production problems this way.

Using the FTE number, instead of actual staffing numbers, allows direct comparisons of several different line conditions: half days, overtime, extra people, or part time employees. The process is to convert all applied hours - the hours worked by the number of people - divided by 8 for a day or shift or by 40 for a week's efforts. Tracking the weekly number will show trends and improvements. When the team leader reviews the numbers each week, he or she has the perfect opportunity to discuss the successes made and the impediments discovered, not just as explanations of the numbers, but as opportunities for instruction or problem solving.

Why will the employees trust this number? They calculate it! One of the first assignments made or, better, volunteers called for, will have several team members trained in calculating the number and reporting it. The team owns the number; it is the result of their demonstrated effort. And the team must calculate the number and be ready to discuss the results.

The results and any discussion are for understanding and education. They are never a club, even when results show a decline. The team will learn the factors that impact their performance. They will learn how to use the numbers to decide how many people are needed for a given output to be maintained or to determine how many more items can be produced in a day or a week when demand makes increased output necessary. Supervisors have the same advantage when asked or tasked by senior management to determine capacity levels. All have real data to base decisions on, instead of trying to do a rough-cut capacity plan on the fly.

This gives real data to the team for the team problem solving efforts described in the next chapter.

Chapter Six – Force Multiplier

Your team building effort is now beginning to pay off. You have told the members many times that they are a team. You and they have changed the way they look at their jobs and their workplace. Your team has confidence in your leadership and you are becoming more relaxed as a leader. Now you can show the team how to solve the problems that frustrate them daily. Often people what to know what going Lean means to them personally. They understand that "management" wants to "cut costs", but how do those on the team benefit?

You must be very upfront about the Lean Initiative. Yes, the organization began this journey and asked everyone to join. Yes, the goal is to make the company more competitive by increasing quality and safely raising productivity. And there are also several direct benefits to all employees. They can resolve issues that have been frustrating them. They can learn more skills. They can learn how to improve processes. They can help create their own job security, since the only job security that anyone really has is that customers continue to demand the products or services the company provides.

Using teams of employees to solve problems is a major contributor to ongoing company health. And the people on these teams must be assured by your plan and reassured by your actions that no one will lose their job as a result of the Lean initiative.

Group problem solving done correctly will add to every team member's experience in a positive way. They will learn that they can reduce some of their frustrations; they will enjoy having their ideas listened to by their peers, team leaders, and supervisors; they will be the authors of successful changes.

There are many problem solving formulas available to teams. I have used a nine-step system for years that works well for complex problems or problems

involving multiple departments or disciplines:
1. State the problem. 2. Identify all possible causes. 3. Identify all possible solutions. 4. Establish criteria to determine the best solution available. 5. Compare all ideas from the first three steps to the criteria. 6. Solve the problem. Done? No! 7. Develop a plan to implement this solution. 8. Implement. 9. Review the results as a team.

To achieve the best results, add the <u>Five Whys</u> to the second step. The Five Whys refers to a technique of asking "Why?" several times in order to get to the root cause of an issue. The second step is the best point in the process to drive as deeply through an issue as possible before the team wastes a lot of time solving the wrong problem. If this step is taken with proper concentration, the rest of the process becomes much simpler.

The Five Whys are absolutely necessary in order to have all participants think deeply and carefully about each step they propose. Here is an example:

What is the problem?

We reject 10% of our product every day.
Why?

There are too many scratches on the surface.
Why?

We handle the product too much.
Why?

The operator has to lift heavy parts from the inbound skid to the production line.
Why?

It's the only way we have of starting production. We have to get these heavy items off of the inbound skid and onto the line one at a time.
Why?

Because the machine cannot self-feed.

See what the team comes up with now, when you ask for proposals for sensible solutions. You should be getting answers that make sense for this operation, such as use an inclined plane to push the product into place. Or, use a scissors lift. Use a crane. Use two people instead of one to position the product. Your final proposed solution might be something like assigning a second person immediately, while asking engineering to study the relative costs of some or all of the other proposed solutions. If the engineer is already on the team, he better understands why this task is important. And your team will see results immediately from these sessions. Either the number of good products increases or it doesn't. Then do the math. If the number of good parts increases, is the increase large enough to offset the cost of an addition person? The team will find out immediately!

Check the before and after U/FTE number! If you increase the cost of people by 10% and reduce handling damage to zero, you can justify the additional expense. And the actual benefit to the company is even greater than break-even, you reduce the amount of non-value-added work. No one has to take time to deal with the scrap reporting and inventory adjustment. No one has to rework the product or take it to the dumpster if it can't be fixed. There will even be a reduction on the amount of times the dumpster has to be emptied each week.

Where do you get the time and talent to solve problems? You create both by changing your mindset. Stopping production is NOT a bad thing if you use the time productively. Rather, it is an investment, no different than stopping the line to replace a slow machine with a faster one. Again, do the math. If you make 10 wazzits an hour to meet your schedule and you stop production for an hour to solve a problem, you lose 10 wazzits from today's schedule. And in our example above, when you solve the rework problem and make 80 good wazzits every day, you ship 400 perfect pieces every week instead of 360, making up for the invested hour's production in just over a day's time. And you have your gain forever. Not bad – 100% shippable product AND no decrease in productivity (Units/FTE). No trade-off of quality for production!

Use your team leaders to start solving problems right away. They can be easily taught how to facilitate a problem solving session. They must follow the formula chosen or agreed upon for everyone, so that internal customers and suppliers can be quickly integrated into even larger problem solving efforts. Use a white board to capture all ideas and answers; walk the team through the steps until a solution is proposed. Your teams are not wasting production time, they are investing it in a future that will be safer, less frustrating, and more productive. Even meeting time and problem solving time will reduce as more problems are solved, more people are trained it thinking about how to solve problems, and problems get resolved on the line in a stand-up meeting without needing a lot of conference room down time.

Chapter 7 – Cell Design

The following is excerpted from an article written by Dave Grubb of David C Grubb Associates, LLC and used with his kind permission:

"While flow is the focus of the cell design, ultimately the improvement focus is on labor content. A reasonable target for each operator within a cell is to be beneficially "working" 90 to 95 percent of the time. Ultimately, each operator needs to have similar cycle times to establish a rhythm within the cell, which will match the required Takt time.

Traditionally, we would want to "balance" the work demands within in the cell, but do not try to obtain balance initially. Design your cell to utilize ...... operators at 90 percent and allow one operator to be only partially loaded rather than evenly dividing the work. Allowing one operator to be lightly loaded will make optimizing of the actual cell easier.

Within work cells, the operators may or may not move between work elements. In some cases, operators might remain at a single position and "hand off" the part to the next operator. In cells where operators move, there are numerous methods of doing that; deciding which of these methods to use is best left to your specific applications. The most common concept of this movement is that of an operator moving around the cell from beginning to end with the same part until complete, in reality has very limited application."

Perhaps the most important idea to be taken from the above is this: Don't try to get everything right the first time. As General George S. Patton so delicately put it: *A good plan violently executed now is better than a perfect plan next week.*

There is no single right way to create a cell. Choose a design that makes sense for your operation, usually designed around a product family. Cells can be U-shaped, L-shaped, straight lines or whatever you need. Cells may have stations or machines that may not be used by every member of the product family. Use common sense, try something, repeat as necessary!

Step 1 Diagram or photograph the existing layout

Step 2 Diagram the new elements to establish the new process sequence
Simplify flow and make it one direction
Reduce product transportation
Determine how you will get inventory to and from the cell
Make the new layout flexible and easy to visually manage

Step 3 Review the proposal:
Make sure the new layout is safe and waste-free:
Have a place for everything required – **5 S**!
Minimize motion and travel - look for Waste
Eliminate lifting

What follows is an actual example of cell design done on the fly over a span of several weeks with no capital money and little production down time. At the start, all operations were batched and separated by function and the shop looked like Figure 1.

Product moved in clearly defined batches from department to department, and this batch size was determined by the first process: cutting rolls of cloth as efficiently as possible for the cutter. No thought was given of customer needs. Serious oversight by supervisors kept the flow of work going. Parts were brought to each area as requested – often after a stock-out.

The old way was not going to work with the newly introduced product, a simple but fast-selling product that needed an immediate capacity increase to meet demand. Production management met with the employees with the most experience making this product, and using a blank sheet of paper, created the first layout to try after a great deal of discussion.

Figure 1 shows the starting point, typical batch production by function. There is no regard for flow of product.

In our first iteration (Figure 2) we simply asked for everyone's input after explaining what we hoped to accomplish: a reduction in lead time for a hot new chair that was selling at a rate unprecedented in our experience. The suggestions that were agreed on were to move the sewing and upholstery functions for the chosen product line to the assembly area to reduce travel time and increase communication.

Batch Manufacturing

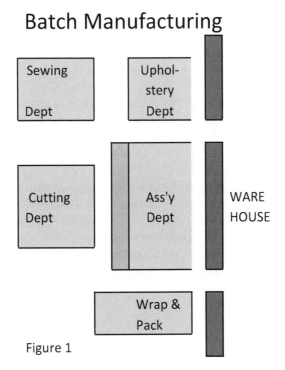

Figure 1

First Iteration

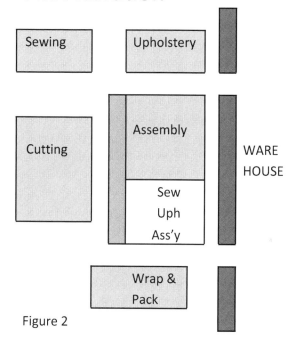

Figure 2

In the area designated in white in Figure 2, we merely moved the standard equipment and work stations from the existing batched departments into this space and began using these stations and tools for the target chair line. We didn't yet have a flow, but we began treating everyone on this line as a true team. Once we had everything together, we quickly understood that changes were necessary to create a real flow.

The subsequent iteration moved the entire cell next to a warehouse wall. Again, a layout was created by consensus of the team, which now included all the people who had worked on this product and the senior material handler from the warehouse. We chose a U-shaped design and included every operation except fabric cutting. (We did not have enough available space for a separate cutting table.) We then established the locations for our Kanbans and our process for maintaining them.

Then, at the suggestion of the material handler, we cut a hole in the warehouse wall and installed some gravity-fed rollers as the Kanban for the bulkiest items required by the cell, the chair frames, saving a lot of travel time for the small warehouse crew and in the process improving Safety by reducing the number of trips for forklifts into the people-filled manufacturing area.

Second Iteration

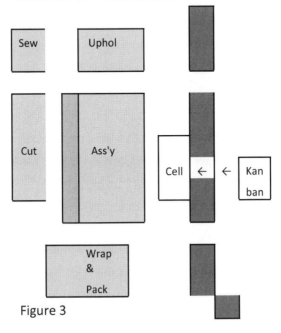

Figure 3

Some extra tools and supplies were purchased in order to have every workstation on the new line completely set up and ready to go whenever the schedule required production from that line. The hourly members of our little *ad hoc* committee quickly decided on their own that they wanted to set up a job rotation, since most individual operations were relatively simple. Figure 4 shows the details of our final layout, including Kanbans.

Cell Design

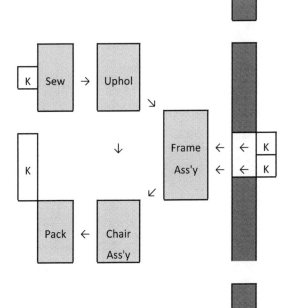

Figure 4

The final iteration turned out to be cultural, not physical. From one to five people were now assigned to the cell depending upon the daily schedule, so communication needed to be quick and transparent to answer the question of "where do we start today?" We created a production white board listing the schedule and staffing with space to record actual output and any issues that arose that were not severe enough to shut down the line.

We established four Kanbans for the area to stage parts. The first accepted the cut covers and was located next to the sewing machine. The next two were the sets of gravity-fed roller conveyers, one with black frames and one with chrome frames. These were monitored from the warehouse side and filled each time there was room for the next box at the convenience of the fork lift driver. The final Kanban was set up next to the aisle for easy access and was a true two-bin system. Any material handler passing by would pick up the empty bins, knowing they had two hours to return with replenishment.

We now cut only one day's worth of covers, not an entire order's worth, and only after a trial cover had been approved from each of the fabrics to be used, since we often were required to use a fabric specified by the customer. Then the sewing machine was raised to standing height, a shock for the sewers! And then the men asked to be trained for sewing the covers so that job rotation was complete, a much bigger shock for everyone! We also instituted quality at the source – no one was to accept substandard work from the station feeding theirs, and anyone could stop the line for a problem. Quality at the Source was instituted without any fanfare or gnashing of teeth. It wasn't a Program or management Buzzword. It was simply the way we were doing things.

The results by the end of the third iteration implementation were better than we could have guessed at the beginning. Shift Capacity increased from 230 to 275 chairs while Staffing decreased from 7 to 5 operators: a 67% increase in productivity. Quick Ship chairs became Make-to-Order products instead of Make-to-Stock – available in any standard fabric or frame finish as lead time dropped from four weeks to three days. Finished goods inventory dropped to zero – products were scheduled to be shipped on the day produced for less-than-truckload quantities. Defective product that got shipped to customers was Zero. After cross-training everyone who worked on this product, flexibility was perfect: any number of people from one to five could make the complete product. And W-I-P inventory no longer piled up wherever an operator had extra parts or time to make product that could not be immediately consumed by the next station.

Since staffing varied with the schedule, we used a simple model to determine the number of people needed for the shift: Calculate Takt time and divide it by the cycle time to determine the number of people needed. Our continuing experience and use of U/FTE calculations taught us when to add the "decimal" person and when to go without.

Oh, did I mention that we did this in a union shop? The people and the shop steward understood that job security, where there is any at all, comes from getting better at everything they do that will help get and keep customers.   The shop steward worked on this line, and since it was our first "showcase" line, we routinely took visiting customers to this line and let them build a chair for themselves, overseen by and interacting with the people on the line. How many union shops do you know of where you could do this? That's why you succeed when you change your own behavior, show others what you expect, then walk the talk.

We benefited greatly from the physical changes that we made, but we benefited even more from the gradual change in the way the operators saw how that line worked. To me, two of the changes were enormous! In nearly twenty years in office furniture factories, I had never seen a sewer stand to work, and I have only ever seen one male sewing machine operator and he was a very special case.

A long-term employee, he contracted MS and could no longer work standing on a concrete floor all day. Our Personnel VP (that's what we called them then) was exceptionally good at thinking outside the box and suggested that the employee move to the sewing department where he would not have to stand and lift all day.

He did and was accepted immediately by the women because they knew his situation. With their help he became a decent sewer and prolonged his working life by a great many years. Again, another example that when you change the culture, you can improve people's work lives.

Chapter 8 - New rules for the organization!

There are new rules for organizations that are adopting Lean. All involve trusting your people to become engaged and constantly strive to do the right thing.

1. It's now YOUR job. It's not just the manager's or supervisor's or line leader's job. Once Continuous Improvement Teams have been chartered with the ownership of the process and product under their control, all members of the teams jointly own the entire effort. Ownership means that, succeed or fail, the Team is responsible for their results and must hold themselves accountable for their performance.

2. 5S is a part of every job description and process. Maintain the organization and presentation of your work area at all times. Update your standard 5 S efforts immediately for every layout, process, or workstation change. Make sure new

taped areas and labels are put in place at once and scrape up all old labels and any tape that no longer designates a needed space. Review and update your Kanbans to reflect the best possible balance of inflow and usage of parts and supplies.

3. Leaders need to remember their own needs:

Breathe. This means "Slow Your Brain Down!" until you are sure you see the real picture in front of you. Even when you need to act or react quickly, do not act hastily! Get your bearings, decide how important or urgent your next step is and act appropriately. Safety issue? Jump right on it! Someone on the line doesn't get that they have to help clean up? Take a deep breath, then take them aside and re-instruct them on their role. Apply proper situational leadership.

Slow down to go faster. Yeah, this is where your team members and teammates laugh when you implore them. You will have to remind them all, until they all understand, that no customer wants a bad item shipped to them, even if it's on time! You are being a good leader when you can tell the team how many of their items have been returned. They need the data as badly as you do in order to correct the process. Slow down to make the product correct every time. Speed will come later. Slow down to fix a problem before an item ships. Slow down or stop to solve the problem so that all future shipments are defect free.

Teach others to do what you need done. If you are a manager or supervisor, you have a great many tasks and priorities. How do you do all that needs to be accomplished every day and find time to coach, problem-solve, and plan? Delegate! Teach your team members to do some of the tasks. Think about which tasks will help them grow professionally or give them insight into the work you are doing? Have them deal with tracking output, cycle times, calculating the units produced per FTE, and tracking improvements in this measure week over week to show productivity gains accomplished by the team. This is a good way to ensure engagement in the team and process, and provides you with the data and experience you need to identify the next generation of Theory L leaders.

Smile. If you are like me, and show your emotions all too easily, learn to smile instead. Smiling sends more than just a signal that you are happy. It signifies your willingness to stand in the middle of your action station, ready for what's coming next. I often ask people the question I once saw as a book title: "What do you say when you talk to yourself?" If you look forward to the next challenge or opportunity, send that signal so your team will understand that together you can climb over or through the next barrier.

Have fun. If it's not fun, you are really not doing Lean or Theory L the right way! You are missing out on many opportunities to learn, grow, teach, and succeed. Why did you get into management, anyway? For the money?

For the unpaid overtime? Or for the chance to do something important and for the opportunity to take a risk and be wrong? It's like being a goalie! Jacques Plante, goalie for the Montreal Canadiens when they won five Stanley Cups in six trips to the finals, once asked, "How would you like to have a job where every time you made a mistake, a red light goes on and 18,000 people boo?" That's management! It's just the other side of the coin; when you make the save, there is no red light and 18,000 people cheer. It's a great feeling.

Lead. This is your opportunity to try all the things you have learned, to actually apply them in the real world with your team. Show others the best way to solve their own problems and reduce their daily frustrations. Improve things for yourself and your organization. Prove to yourself and to everyone around you that you not only know how to lead, but that in fact you have the right stuff to make things happen.

4. Use your new tools to solve the problems you encounter as you work to eliminate waste and frustration from your workday. Remember that Continuous Improvement goes on forever, an integral part of everyone's job every day. Managers and supervisors must meet with teams, seek out their input on both the problems and the solutions, then lead the team through the problem solving

5. Anyone can stop any process. This isn't just for production lines, either. If the process is broken or no longer yielding the expected results, those involved must stop what they are doing and fix the process. People must understand that this is their responsibility! Don't wait for the boss. Don't keep working hoping the process will fix itself. Stop what you're doing and fix it. Quality at the Source is not a chapter title - it is the new culture.

6. Become Theory L leaders: Find, recruit, and train more leaders so that the

organization continues to improve and be successful.

Chapter Nine – Syncing Inventory, the Back Office, and Shipping with Production

Now you are ready to integrate your production schedule with your shipping schedule. Since you can make product more quickly and at a higher level of quality, you no longer need the buffer of a Finished Goods Inventory to ensure on-time shipments. You know how long it takes to load a truck, so you only have to have the order ready to ship the day before, not a week or two before to allow rework to catch up.

Use Takt time and your new cycle times to schedule your production to start the number of days or hours before shipment. Of course this will make everyone nervous, but as with everything else we've discussed, you can do this in iterations that slowly thrust you out of your comfort zone without scaring everyone involved. You will get it to work for you because you have already built a great deal of credibility in your new vision by the work already accomplished.

You will need to do some prep work. Your Bills of Material must be correct. You cycle times must be known and stable. You must convince the schedulers not to sneak in any "just in case" time. If you do need to provide a buffer at first to protect customer delivery dates, do so at the finished goods level. That way you will prove your cycle times and processes are correct, and as everyone watches the pile of finished product grow, they will very quickly see that time from production start to shipment can be safely reduced. And then quickly remove the excess finished goods. If it is finished, it ought to be on a truck headed to a customer so you can get paid, right? So it is the best visual signal.

The most important benefit, however, is in having the time at first to solve the issues that will come with the change in the process. It gives you a little time to breathe while everyone learns the new process and what to expect from it.

Again, if it does nothing except reduce the fear of the unknown or the fear of failure, improving by degrees pays for itself.

I would suggest that this is the best time for Tom Peters' ready-fire-aim approach. Do NOT wait for all bills and routings to be correct. Get started and tackle these issues as they arise. You've got the time now, you quality is high, your set up and processing time is greatly reduced. All of the previous efforts will pay off now.

Get the people involved with these processes engaged in their own Lean thinking. Kaizen efforts and spaghetti charts work for every process, not just on an assembly line. You can reduce "paper" processing time, eliminate redundancy, reduce errors, and increase inventory accuracy the same way you improved manufacturing productivity. Create continuous improvement teams in the office and on the shipping dock.

And create a Lean warehouse! Your warehouse has to support the improvements in production, so you must create the necessary climate there: 5 S, productivity measurements (yes, really), team approach, continuous improvement. How? Take everything you've just learned and apply it to the warehouse. The warehouse effort will mirror the rest of the results, with the added benefit of improved inventory storage and usage, and improved inventory accuracy.

Every part of your enterprise will benefit from Lean thinking.

Chapter 10 -The Most Dreaded Phase of Lean: The Pull System!

I watched a young supervisor, who with hands on hips and a scowl on his face, surveying his line of semi-custom product, watching while the Inch Worm devoured his flow. He studied the line quite a while and then confessed that he couldn't find his true bottleneck. It kept moving! From one end of the line to the other and back again, the product would randomly pile up before breaking loose and moving toward the take-off station.

You have all experienced the Inch Worm. Just like the little green bug, it sits in your line and moves back and forth as more product is started on the line than can be finished. Sensing an excellent teaching moment, I asked the supervisor if he had thought about possible causes for the moving bottleneck and talked them over with those on the line. No, he said, he needed to study it longer so he could figure it out. I asked how he planned to do that and learned that he had no plan beyond watching. That's when I decided to accelerate his education.

Through a series of questions I helped him create a plan to generate some data to be considered and some steps to take, starting with calling a team meeting. I explained that as a Lean Leader, his goal was to use his entire team to measure output, discover ways to improve their process, and eliminate rework. Team members must understand what is expected of them if they are to begin to change their attitudes and behaviors. They must learn how to take time studies and observe flow. They can use spaghetti charts to determine wasted movement and transportation to eliminate time and steps in the process, shorten production lines and do all the other steps necessary to get ready for the biggest step of all.

When you have eliminated the rest of the waste from your line, have rebalanced the line and relayed out the line to accommodate the new process, and have realigned your Kanbans, then it's time once more to return the team to the meeting room and discuss the most radical, frightful, fateful Lean idea of all - a Pull System!

This is another opportunity for Theory L leaders to create "Aha" moments for their teams and the leaders they are training. And this is why you always carry a string or small piece of chain in your pocket! Gather everyone together around a bench or table, then take out your string and lay it flat, and ask someone to push the string in a straight line. They can't. Ask someone else to try. After a good laugh, ask one of the same people to pull the string. Now talk to them again about a pull system versus a push system. As always, elicit ideas from the team and help them answer their questions. Guide the team to talking themselves out of any fears they might have.

Even better, create or buy one of the games that simulate a production process that starts with "batch" manufacturing and piles of inventory and leads to the Lean solution for those playing it. These have been around for a long time - HP had one they used the mid-Eighties! - and I have watched while Operations VP's, production managers and hourly employees reached "Aha!" moments. The hourly folks usually figure it out before the executives, so start with execs who are not thin-skinned!

Why is the step to a Pull System so rarely (at least in my experience) taken? Most production guys like to know how well they've done for the day, week, or month, how many UNITS they produced. We've all learned that if you can't build it, you can't ship it. If you can't ship it, you can't invoice for it. Given our years of experience at this, the last thing we understand is STOPPING PRODUCTION! Yes, indeed! The Pull System stops production, makes workers wait, and of course it WON'T WORK with OUR product or OUR people or OUR process.

The Pull System will result in additional waste at first. There <u>will</u> <u>be</u> people standing around if their customer has no place to move their product to, though how this is worse than the delays caused by the inch worm escapes me. You see, with a pull system you will now quickly find Herbie, Dr. Goldratt's bottleneck! You can now do a final re-balance of the line and restore your flow.

If you do not know Herbie, I suggest that you obtain a copy of <u>The Goal</u> by Eli Goldratt.
This groundbreaking book on The Theory of Constraints is the first book I give to new supervisors and Continuous Improvement Team facilitators. For a book that has been around for thirty-plus years, it offers timely thoughts and ideas about managing with people.

Wow! Would there really be no immediate improvement to output for switching to a pull system? No! The improvement will be immediate and will grow quickly as you apply your Lean tools to the reconstituted process. With the demise of the infamous Inch Worm, any hiccups in the flow become obvious and can be jumped on by the team and resolved quickly because they are no longer hidden from view. W-I-P disappears as the Inch Worm is eliminated. Finished Goods is the only inventory of value; move it immediately to Shipping! You will begin to see more Finished Goods for the effort of labor and material you expend, and Finished Goods are the only inventory you can invoice for. Clients won't willingly pay to let you build incomplete product.

As with the majority of technical changes, the pull system by itself is subject to failure only from the people side. If the team has done its homework prior to this step, it's most likely that the technical issues are all out of the way. The question becomes - has the team sufficiently trained itself for the new behaviors? Try it! Set up the new line with a completed item at each station.

With everyone else watching, have the people at the take-off station remove the finished product, opening up their inbound Kanban for the next finished product. Walk the process back up the line until those at the beginning have nothing in front of them. Now let them go to work. Watch the line carefully to ensure that the process is followed and no additional product is worked on at any station. As the team gets used to it and establishes the flow, carefully observe to see if Herbie returns. If he does, the team can quickly resolve the causes that led to it.

Leave time at the end of the first day to allow the team to share feelings as well as observations and results. Discuss all the concerns openly and make a plan to address them the next day. Repeat as necessary! Be sure to ask a volunteer to tally daily and weekly results to show the improvement made in quality and productivity. Ideally, your team will already be tracking its Units/FTE and the numbers will quickly prove the results.

Chapter 11 - Don't Hold Back!

Throughout the process of implementing Lean, people will find their own "Aha" moments. Watch for these so you can encourage the right behavior for that moment. I watched while a Division Manager pulled this off perfectly when a young supervisor reached his moment.

The Division Manager was in the plant for the day and as usual was practicing the fine art of Managing by Wandering Around. As he approached the young supervisor's line, he stopped to listen to an impromptu Team Meeting as the members discussed the amount of time spent walking between two stations. Someone suggested that they simply move the workstations closer together to create a literal hand-off, and when everyone agreed, another crew member asked how long it would take maintenance to do it. The supervisor replied that the crew could do it themselves and asked when would be the best time. The Crew saw the Division Manager step in as he asked, "Who owns this line?" and the young supervisor claimed it. Then he repeated his claim and included the entire crew. What happened next surprised some of the team members.

The Division Manager simply said, "Let's go!" With the Division Manager pitching in, the workstations were moved in twenty minutes. The Division Manager let the crew take a few minutes to celebrate. I still have the picture on my phone.

The best part of this story is that the team later combined the two workstations into one and shortened both the physical distance of travel as well as the time, and allowed two crew members to be moved to new line where their experience was needed. Their jobs were secure and the company did not have to hire two new people.

We live in a world of instant gratification, so why not make the most of it. When you can do something now, just do it! It satisfies the excitement of those who helped and sends the right messages to your supervisor and the employees. It means that now is better than later. It means you will allow the teams some leeway in taking a risk and back them up if they fail. And it's OK to fail.

Lean implementation gets to be fun for everyone at this level. Most of us get a real kick out of fixing something, making things better, making work simpler and less frustrating. Too often in the past, only those of us at managerial or executive levels got to play with the "what-ifs" and "why-nots." We used to ignore ideas that our employees had. If the company we worked in was big enough to have industrial engineers, we could let them consider new layouts, but rarely did anyone else do it. Now everyone gets a chance.

I was invited to visit a near-by plastics molding company that instituted a drive toward Lean and brought in a new Plant

Manager to head the operation. He began the usual Lean training and education for all his people and he also did a lot of MBWA, Management by Wandering Around: observing the processes; seeing the problems; selling the new philosophy; and listening, listening, listening. One particular operator collared him and took him on a tour of his part of the shop. The operator complained that even though he cleaned the area every day, it was trashed and messed up when he arrived every morning. The people who did the same job he did on the other two shifts didn't work the way he did and would not listen to his suggestions because he wasn't the boss. Then he related that he had spoken to all three shift supervisors but to no avail.

Using this incident as a special opportunity to teach, the Plant Manager quickly set about training his supervisors to think and manage differently, teaching them better communication skills as well as Lean techniques. In a year he had transformed this factory by staying on message, by supporting training and by listening to all employees. The factory broke even for the first time in several years. The following year it was making money again.

Oh, and the brave employee who spoke his mind? He devised a way to accomplish his department's tasks on just one shift, with considerably less waste of material, and in a much more orderly fashion. The operators on the other two shifts were reassigned. I have seen his work area and it is very clean and organized, the epitome of 5S!

Great story, right? And the most important leadership quality was the manager's ability to stay on message. His relentless pursuit of this goal was the catalyst for the entire plant to accomplish this effort.

Whether studying, teaching, or practicing Lean, you will see and hear many such stories. Their meaning is simple: people will follow the leaders they trust, and will often surprise you with their quick adoption of the new behaviors.

I have led many problem sessions centered on line layout, and in both union and non-union shops. The results all go in the right direction. If you have built the trust and earned the respect of the people, you can watch as they willingly follow your leadership. Once they are willing to follow, you then teach them to lead. This is your "Aha" moment, when you can see how much more you can accomplish with enthusiastic individuals and teams directing their own improvement efforts.

Chapter 12 - Lean Forever

I hope by now that I have convinced you that Lean Leadership is the best way to create a Lean implementation that can be sustained for the long haul. The culture you create will provide the mindset that everyone in the organization is responsible for their own attitudes and behaviors that lets them become willing participants in your Lean philosophy.

You have seen the fantastic results that can be achieved by good leaders and trained, motivated self-directed work teams. Keep looking for the next class of leaders and teach them everything you've learn, including how to spot future leaders. Keeping the strength and spirit of Theory L leaders flowing through your organization will give you the best chance to succeed in the years ahead.

A consulting engineer once told me that he thought Just-In-Time could be defined as the Relentless Pursuit of Housekeeping, and it worked for him and the people he led. I think the most important part is "relentless" and not housekeeping or 5 S, because it means staying on message. I can't think of a stronger tool for a leader to use.

People are the key to any implementation, whether Lean, ERP, or starting a new product line. Find leaders who are good with people and who can be trained to find other leaders to keep good ideas and improvements cascading through the organization.

Lean must become the way of life for all those involved. When I am asked how far along a company needs to be to consider itself Lean, I respond with "When It's Lean, It's Routine!" You really do reach this point. When your culture supports the behaviors required to perform to the new way of working, you are Lean. You have led your people to become willing contributors to the change, to solving their own problems, and to stepping up in leadership roles throughout your organization.

Lean is the attitude or philosophy that sets your organization apart from all others and your job is to use your Theory L leaders to continue these efforts – forever.

About the author

Alan Severance is the senior operations and manufacturing resource for the Riverton Management Consulting Group, with a successful track record of innovative and cost-effective solutions to business problems. With his strong leadership skills and experience, he has led cross-functional teams to accomplish continuous improvement of processes and product.

His experience includes leading several transformative initiatives to support market changes, integrating Sales and Operations Planning processes to ensure a consistent company-wide approach to business planning, and leading successful Lean implementations. Consequently, he is skilled in structuring organizations to effectively address current and future market requirements, as well as recruiting, training, and leading multi-disciplinary professionals to deliver high value returns on investment.

Alan's projects have helped companies improve productivity and reduce cost through his development of Theory L Leadership, a people-centered approach to LEAN Manufacturing that emphasizes creating and empowering leaders who train others to lead.

Corporate Alignment and Lean solutions are key to successful growth and continuous improvement of manufacturing companies. The global economy revolves around the health of the manufacturing sectors and Alan knows and has researched methods that create a vibrant manufacturing business.

A graduate of Hamilton College, Alan earned his MBA in Organization and Management from Temple University, Philadelphia, PA. He and his wife currently live in southeastern Pennsylvania.

Alan always welcomes your feedback on these ideas and wants to hear of your successes and challenges. Please contact him at alseverance13@msn.com with your suggestions and questions.

Made in the USA
Middletown, DE
20 September 2019